God's Purpose

For My Pain

God's Purpose For My Pain

by Pastor Jerome G. Farris

Editors

Ray Glandon
Trudy Mosley

Senior Publisher

Trudy Mosley

Awarded Publishing House

ASA Publishing Company

A Publisher Trademark Title page

ASA Publishing Company
Awarded Best Publisher for Quality Books

(Wayne Commerce Park)
38640 Michigan Avenue, Wayne, Michigan 48184
www.asapublishingcompany.com

Copyrights©2009 Jerome G. Farris, All Rights Reserved
Book: God's Purpose For My Pain
Date Published: 11.23.09 /Edition 1 *Trade Paperback*
Book ASAPCID: 2380526
ISBN: 978-0-9841442-8-0
Library of Congress Cataloging-in-Publication Data

This book was published in the United States of America.
State of Michigan

A Publisher Trademark Title page

In memory of my beloved wife, Helene.
You are my inspiration in seeking the
greater purpose God has for me in
making a difference in the
lives of others.

I dedicate this book to you
and the love we shared together.

2   *Pastor Jerome G. Farris*

Contents

4   *Pastor Jerome G. Farris*

FOREWORD

Death is never something we get used to, and when it hits so close to home, it can be even more difficult to accept. Because of the closeness of our relationship to Pastor Farris and Sister Farris, when my wife, Janice and I heard the news that Helene had gone home to be with the Lord, and knowing how much they loved each other, his pain became "our pain."

I struggled during these last few months wondering whether I had done enough in letting my brother know I loved him. Being the impulsive man that I am, I wanted to be there more than I was, but the Spirit of God wouldn't let me. I may have gotten in the way and tried to make him heal quicker than he should have. I thank God for His Spirit.

Yes, it's good to have family and friends around, but the reality is that there will be times when you find that you are all alone... no one but you and God. Healing is a process, a process between you and God. It is something that God must do from within to that person who is hurting. Healing takes time, and not everyone will heal the same way. You hear so much about how the Lord moves in mysterious ways. When my brother said that the Lord would not allow him to sleep, that he was told to write down what he was feeling to cope with his pain, and how it had now turned into a book, I became very excited. To see how God would use Pastor Farris' struggles to help others became very encouraging to me.

God's Purpose For My Pain will allow you to see one man's love, one man's pain, God's purpose for the pain, and God's grace in healing that pain. As God has used Pastor Farris in this most uniquely transparent way, listen to God's voice, and let Him show you how you can be used in comforting those who will experience loss in their lives. Also know that God is there in any "dark period of our lives" with the same reassurance that He cares. I have been tremendously blessed by this book, and my prayer is that you will, too.

We will miss you, Sister Farris, but we know that your spirit will be in our hearts always. God knows what He is doing. We know everything will be all right. May God bless you, Pastor Farris. May God keep you, and may He bring peace upon you as only He can.

Your Friend, Your Brother,
Reverend Arthur C. Willis Sr., Pastor
Pentecostal Baptist Church
Romulus, Michigan

INTRODUCTION

The decision to document this journey that I am now on was given to me by God.

As I look back now at God's plan for my life, Helene's death has refined my purpose in life. Through the acquaintances and interactions of loved ones coming to see about me and my family at this time, God has used them in so many marvelous ways to help me see and experience Him in ways I never before have. I now know that there is a purpose for the process of grief.

Of all the grief counseling I have done over 19 years of pastoral ministry, to family members, friends and members of my church congregation, no experience has ever taken me to a level so devastating as this one that began on August 5, 2009 at 8:53 a.m. I am thankful to God that when it comes to having lost a loved one, I will be able to share with others just what God can do.

Some may disagree with this statement, but there is no other relationship on earth deeper than that of a husband and wife. God said himself in Genesis 2:23 ***"Therefore shall a man leave his father and his mother, and cleave unto his wife: and the two shall become one flesh."***

Because my love for my wife Helene was so strong and deep, my pain and grief are also very strong and deep. In order for me to be able to move on and continue with my life as I know

Helene would have wanted me to, I could not escape this process but had to go through this valley to reach that mountain of healing.

The purpose of sharing my experience is twofold: first, to show the grace and healing power of God, and second, to help someone else who may take this journey have a better understanding of grief, thereby developing a closer relationship with God.

I have received permission from those whose names are mentioned and therefore thank them for allowing God to use them in ministering to me in this time. Scripture passages are referenced along the way that God gave me as an assurance of His presence and the promise that He would keep me from falling.

I will be eternally grateful to those, who through various means, gave me encouragement and hope. There were some individuals who I believe were sent to me by God to minister to a specific need that I had at various times of this journey. I have called each of them my "angel".

Because we are all individuals, each of us will handle grief differently. This is "my journey". It is a day by day account of things I experienced. At the end of each day, I've listed the emotions I experienced. There is no explanation why there were such extremes — I'm just human.

Grief is an emotion as are anger and guilt. Because we are given emotions by God, experiencing them is natural and healthy. The significance of the experience, however, is knowing that there is a desired end to it by God, called "purpose." For example, guilt has a designed "purpose." Guilt should bring about confession, forgiveness, and ultimately, restoration and peace. On the other hand, if guilt is not dealt with properly according to God's design, it can develop into depression, isolation and misery. The former resolution ensures a good healthy relationship with God... the latter, the disconnection from God. I believe God wants all of us to be at peace with Him. He, and He alone has the answer to all of life's challenges because He "is" the answer to all of life's challenges.

I acknowledge that this journey is one that everyone will have to take but may not experience in the same way as I have. I pray that it will be helpful to you when you have found yourself beginning that journey down the dark road of loss.

10   *Pastor Jerome G. Farris*

"GOD'S PURPOSE FOR MY PAIN"

And we know that all things work together for the good to them that love God, to them who are the called according to his purpose.
Romans 8:28

12　*Pastor Jerome G. Farris*

1

I'm Not Ready

It began.......

August 5, 2009 – Wednesday – 8:53 a.m.

This is the day my life changed forever. My life, love, confidant, and friend for 28 years died and went home to be with the Lord. Even though the sun shined, it was a very dark day.... a day I will always remember.... a day I had wished was just a dream where God would soon awaken me. Family and friends arrived at Providence Hospital. I don't know what I would have done if my brother, Pastor Willis, had not been there and taken charge. When I finally left the hospital and arrived home that afternoon, Mother Rylander, our spiritual mother, and friend, said to me – "Remember what you just preached on Sunday from Psalm 22, God was preparing you for this time."

When mother met me in my kitchen and spoke these words, I politely smiled and respectfully acknowledged her words of encouragement, but at the time I did not care to hear that. I smile now at the incident, for little did I know that God had planted a seed in my spirit that would later produce spiritual fruit for me and others. A lot of people came to the house that day. All I remember was that I was in a daze.... so many people, yet I felt alone. Prayer was offered to the family, and everyone eventually left. I don't know what time it was that night, but I finally laid down on the bed but did not sleep at all. **Emotions experienced: Disbelief, Shock, Numbness.**

So shall my word be that goeth forth out of my mouth, it shall not return unto me void, but it shall accomplish that which I please, and it shall prosper in the thing whereto I sent it.
Isaiah 55:11

August 6 – Thursday

I got up around 1:00 a.m. and began writing Helene's obituary. So much to be said about this beautiful, loving, caring, gifted woman of God with whom I was so blessed to have shared my life. Beginning early that morning, people came to give their condolences. A good friend, Pastor Rodger Hunt, my angel that day, came by. As we shared, that seed spoken of yesterday by Mother began to germinate within me. Looking at Psalms 22 and the question by David, and later quoted by Jesus on Calvary to God of "why have thou forsaken me", I realized that although it appeared God was absent, He was very much with both of us that morning. Even though I needed a miracle from Him to revive Helene, God was at work "behind the scene" fulfilling His promise of eternal life to her, and later I will see His purpose for me. I could not be mad at God, but instead praise Him for what He had done. **Emotions experienced: Disbelief. Gratefulness for His re-**

vealed grace. Numbness. Confusion. Encouragement.

My God, my God, why hast thou forsaken me?
Why art thou so far from helping me and
from the words of my roaring?
But thou art holy, O thou that inhabitest
the praises of Israel.
Psalm 22: 1,3

August 7 – Friday

This morning I had an appointment to go to the cemetery to make arrangements. I needed someone to go with me but could not find anyone. This was the first of many lessons this journey would teach — that this walk will at times be a lonely walk. When my son Gene and his family arrived from Ypsilanti early that afternoon, my 5 year old granddaughter Dariana leaped into my arms. I squeezed her with all that was in me as my thoughts immediately went to Helene. I broke down as I embraced her. Oh how Helene cherished our grandchildren. I thank God that the twins were born prematurely, giving her an opportunity to see them and love on them. Pastor Jake Gaines came by and greatly encouraged me. Another good friend in the ministry, Pastor Columbus Mann offered these words. "In the midst of it all, not understanding why, simply know that God loves you." It was not what was said by these men of God, but how it was said at the time that was so profound and helpful. More family and friends came by, but I needed to get away, so I got on my motorcycle and took a ride. Tears flowing, I had to cut my ride short to prevent a possible accident. Helene and I loved riding together. Later, a situation with my youngest son Dion began to escalate causing great anxiety within the family. I went through the rest of the day somewhat in a daze. **Emotions experienced: Stress. Depression. Encouragement. Numbness. Disbelief.**

.... a time to keep silence, a time to speak.
Ecclesiastes 3:7

August 8 – Saturday

Today I went to the funeral home to make arrangements. I shared with my sister Gloria some personal feelings of hurt I was experiencing. Thank you Gloria for always unconditionally loving me and   being there for me. Much thanks to my sister Muriel and niece Danielle for being with me at this time. I was there ... but not there. It rained that day. **Emotions experienced: Anger. Confusion. Numbness. Disbelief. Depression.**

August 9 – Sunday

Because "church" is who we are, I had to be at my church this morning. This was a very difficult time. As I arrived in the parking lot, I was met and consoled by several members. Clearly, there was a very solemn spirit among the members as everyone greeted us. The magnitude of Helene's passing was tremendous. I spoke privately to our youth minister and his wife, sharing with them the importance of things continuing as Helene would have wanted. I asked Sister Ruffin to take on some of the responsibilities that Helene had overseeing the annual Women's Day and weekly teaching ministry with the women. My church family, all angels that day, were awesome as they surrounded me in love and shared with me in grief. A day of great sorrow, but praises went up to God nevertheless. I want to thank God for the following friends: Pastor Darryl Gaddy, Ron Twymon, Mandee Ham and Annette Lee who worked tirelessly today behind the scenes getting some details for Helene's home going together for me. **Emotions experienced: Numbness. Emptiness. Tremendous Grief. Gratitude and Thanksgiving.**

And whether one member suffer, all members suffer with it; or one member be honored, all the members rejoice with it. Now ye are the body of Christ, and members in particular.
I Corinthians 12:26-27

August 10 – Monday

Another night of little sleep. My family and I went to view Helene's body. As I entered the funeral home chapel, the walk ahead towards Helene was probably the most difficult 40 feet I've ever walked. By now I am so exhausted that I had to ask my nephew Chuck to take me home while the rest of the family remained.

Helene and I always sought God's purpose for us in everything and in everyone we met. Helene had grown very fond of and close to Diane, our grandchildren's other grandmother. "D" as she is so fondly known, being Catholic, and finding out that we were Christians from our son Gene, had a lot of questions about the faith. Helene looked forward to being able to share with her what we know about our God. In Helene's absence I was now blessed to witness to "D" of God's grace and purpose even in Helene's death and how He was going to show Himself in a powerful way in the next couple of days. I talked with family on how I wanted them to deal with my son Dion and his special situation. I grew very concerned how Dion was coping with his mother's passing and believe that a lot of what was going on with him had to do with his inability to deal with what had happened. Around 6:00 p.m. we arrived at the church for the Family Hour. I was very moved by the many people who came that night to give respect and tribute to Helene. I was especially blessed to see Sister Bertile Paterson, 93 years old and one of Helene's childhood spiritual mothers who came all the way from Louisiana. Thank you Marie for going down and bringing her home to be with us. **Emotions experienced: Grief. Hurt. Anger. Stress. Love. Encouragement. Gratefulness. Exhaustion.**

August 11 – Tuesday
HOME GOING SERVICE
I do not believe this is really happening. I am about to see my best friend, my heart, my breath, my love for the last time here. As we arrive at the church, to see the tremendous outpouring of people is overwhelming. Momma's home going was wonderful, but this service is

like none I had ever witnessed. There was so much love shown. So many wonderful things said about Helene. So many people whose lives she touched. Pastor Willis conducted the service with such grace and dignity. Debbie Johnson, Helene's childhood friend, gave a wonderful tribute of how Helene's *"little four foot nine inch body could no longer contain her desire to minister to others and serve God."* Pastor J.H. Johnson, my pastor, delivered a powerful eulogy. His testimony of Helene was that her eulogy would not be preached because her eulogy was lived. She believed in the Word of God and therefore believed...

For our light affliction,
which is but for a moment, worketh
for us a far more exceeding and eternal weigh of glory.
While we look not at the things which are seen, but
at the things which are not seen: for the things
which are seen are temporal; but the
things which are not seen are eternal.
2 Corinthians 4: 17-18

Helene and I had such a wonderfully open relationship. We talked about everything, even when this time would come and what our desires were. We knew that one of us would eventually leave the other behind. Her desire was to have a graveyard ceremony, something that you don't see much of anymore. If there would be anyone who could make it special, it would be Pastor Willis.

I will always remember **"If I were to preach, I would preach....."** Helene had to have been looking down smiling on us.   It was just the way I believe she had envisioned it to be.

Later, when we got home from the repast, Diane asked me a question that not only caused me to smile but to shout "Hallelujah," which startled her. She asked what would she need to do to become "Baptist." I told her simply to believe in the Lord Jesus Christ and be baptized.   That night, after everyone had gone home, I retired but could not sleep. I found myself reliving moment by moment one week ago leading to Helene's passing, looking at what I should have done to prevent her from leaving me. These same thoughts came at the hospital, and I was told, "It would not have mattered what you did. God had it planned, it went according to His plan, and that was it. There was nothing you could have done to change it. Don't beat yourself up. You did all you could." I tried desperately to remember the last time I told her I loved her, but could not   remember.   **Emotions   experienced: Numbness. Encouragement. Love. Praise and Thanksgiving. Guilt and Regret. Exhaustion.**

2

No Need To Go On

August 12 – Wednesday

Had a restless night. I got up early and took a ride to the cemetery on my motorcycle. What a beautiful sunny and warm day it was. I sat there at Helene's grave site for a while. Because I felt so alone and needed to be with family, I had to see Gene and the babies, so I took a ride to Ypsilanti. Once I arrived, I embraced the children and told them how much I loved them. It was a very emotional time as I stood in the babies' bedroom observing how wonderfully decorated it was and that Helene would not be here to see her babies grow up. We never know from one day to the next what a day will bring. I told Gene and Robyn not to let a day go by where you do not say to each other "I Love You." I returned home late that night. It was very difficult walking in the house and not being greeted at the door with a kiss by my wife as I was always accustomed. **Emotions experienced: Loneliness. Joy. Sadness. Regret. Depression.**

August 13 – Thursday

The feeling of loneliness and Helene not coming back really began to set in. Satan began to attack my mind. I could not be alone. Went by my sister Deborah's house. Spent some time with my mother. Received a call from a member grieving over Helene's death who expressed that he "needed his pastor." As a Pastor, it is a natural instinct to reach out and help the hurting. We store a reservoir of God's Word and His grace to use in times like these for others. But at this time, I found that I had nothing to give anyone. My response to this member was …. no response. Realizing I was on empty myself, I had no words of comfort. God would send me people who understood where I was and what I was going through.

The first was Pastor Jerome McAfee who just 3 months ago lost his wife. Our conversation was very uplifting as he shared with me what he found was helping him in this process. His advice was having family and friends around, and if possible, getting away for a while. I left my sister's house around 7:00 p.m. and went by Marie Turner's to see Sister Paterson before she went back home to Louisiana. Arrived home about 9:30 p.m. **Emotions experienced: Loneliness. Fear. Guilt. Encouragement.**

August 14 – Friday

Another night of little sleep. I woke up again with Helene on my mind. Helene was always concerned about making sure that I had something to eat. Everyone knows that she was an excellent cook. She made sure that even in her absence, others would ensure that I ate something. I thank God for my youngest sister Cecilia. She has personally taken on the responsibility of making sure that I have something to eat as well as any other things that Helene would have done at home for me. I know Helene is looking down from heaven with gratitude to my sister for filling in and taking care of me.

A high school classmate and friend, Chris, came by, and spent the whole day with me. He took me to his house where we looked at a couple of movies, ate, and really relaxed until around 5:30 p.m. For a few hours it seemed like I was in another world, until I got back home and reality set in. Satan began to attack my mind with thoughts of depression. I began to think of no longer caring any more about God's purpose for me, now that Helene was gone. The church and the mission were no longer top priorities. I did not care about anything, and nothing mattered anymore. I recognized Satan at work.

Satan's objective is to, in anyway he can, discredit God. Because he cannot touch God, he tries the next best thing, and that is, go after those whom God loves, and that is us. Satan would want my testimony damaged by losing faith and forgetting all I have dedicated these past 19 years in teaching and preaching.

I began to understand that God was in control of this situation and that His purpose was at work. I'm reminded of Job and how Satan was allowed to bring chaos into Job's life, hoping that Job would "curse God and just die." Job lost so much and was so low but still could say *"though he slay me, yet will I trust Him..."* I am a witness that God knows what you need when you need it.

He had another high school friend, my angel that day named Wendell, call me and express concern about me being idled too long giving Satan a foothold in trying to cause havoc and damage to my testimony. I give reference to something I later read in a book I was blessed with by a friend concerning the process of grief that stated *"the greatest tribute to the life of a loved one who is gone is to continue in the work that person was so passionate about."*

Helene loved the church, the people of God, the children and those less fortunate. The enemy will seek to take advantage in our times of weakness. How important it is that the others see in me my faith at work. Because of God's call on my life as a leader, my testimony especially now needed to be consistent with what I know to be true. I am not immune to the process nor to the natural tendencies that can be experienced as a man, but I also acknowledge my responsibility to others in proclaiming the hope that we have in our risen Savior Jesus Christ.

If there be no resurrection from the dead,
then Christ is not risen:
And if Christ be not risen, then is
our preaching in vain
and your faith is also vain.
I Corinthians 15:13-14

At this time I had no strength of my own. I

was weak and very vulnerable to the weaknesses of the flesh, and if my faith was to be evident to others, God would have to step in and do something at this time. **Emotions experienced: Fear. Numbness. Disconnection from God. Guilt. Gratitude for family and friends. Encouragement. Denial.**

August 15 - Saturday

Surprisingly, I was able to get a good night of sleep. Still somewhat in a daze, I went out to lunch with some high school classmates. Later, I went to the show with another dear friend. I find myself still under attack. **Emotions experienced: Guilt. Grateful for friends – took mind off Helene for a while. Disconnection from God.**

August 16 - Sunday

I went to church this morning. Our youth minister preached a wonderful sermon. I had to apologize to the member who had called in need of comforting for possibly being insensitive but would share with him now the words from Psalm 27:10 that *"When my father and my mother forsake me, then the Lord will take me up."* There will be times in our lives when even those you depend on will let you down, but always remember that God will always be there for you.

> *.....for he hath said, I will never leave thee*
> *nor forsake thee.*
> *Hebrews 13:5b*

I received a letter in the mail from Sister

Deborah Daniels, a beautiful saint in the Lord who understood what I was now experiencing due to having just lost her husband one year ago.

Satan is really after me now with impure thoughts I know are not of God. **Emotions experienced: Grief. Loneliness. Depression. Praise. Fear. Guilt.**

August 17 – Monday

Not sure what time I got up this morning. I thought it would be good for me to get back into a routine. I went to work. Totally numb and in a daze, I realized I could not stay. I left work and came back home. Dwain Phelps, a friend of my sister Deborah came by, and brought me a book *When Grief Breaks Your Heart*, by James W. Moore. This book was a tremendous blessing that ministered to me in understanding the process. I read it a couple of times today. Thank you Dwain. I went to bed late. **Emotions experienced: Numbness. Depression. Loneliness. Guilt.**

August 18 – Tuesday

I woke up this morning around 3:45 a.m. Another night of little sleep. Received a long distant phone call from a good friend, Pastor Gabriel Lewis from Orlando Florida. He shared with me some personal experiences that he had gone through and how God helped him when darkness entered his life. As I went on through the morning I began to experience a cloud of depression and grief. It was at this time that the phone rang, and it was another friend, Pastor Carl Graham. God's angel for me that day shared with me how God had helped and strengthened him when he had lost his wife some seven years ago. What helped him most of all was praising God. I came to discover that by praising God despite your pain, the load and burden of what you are experiencing is transferred, if, but for a moment, to one who is able and who cares. The focus is shifted from you to who God is. Because of who He is and the fact that He cares for me, when this process is over, what fruit that will be produced will be for my good and His glory.

> *Cast your cares upon him,*
> *for he carest for you.*
> *1 Peter 5:7*

I have discovered that part of the healing process is the closure. Helene had a number of physical illnesses, and I had to know exactly what happened. I received by mail an autopsy of her death. My baby was really sick, more than she wanted me to know. She was never one who complained but always pressed her way through her own challenges and "pain" to help others and do what was needed to be done.

As her husband, I vowed before God that I would protect her. I always sought within my power to shield her from external things and pressures of life that could harm her. It really hurts when you know that there are just some things that are outside of your power to do. This was one of those things that grieved me so. I hated when she was in pain and I could do nothing about it. I would have without a thought taken on myself all her pain. **Emotions experienced: Encouragement. Grief. Depression. Acknowledgment of Sin and thankful for forgiveness. Guilt. Helplessness.**

3

Picking Up The Pieces

August 19 – Wednesday

I woke up this morning about 4:30 very depressed. Received a call from Mother Lillian Rogers, a dear friend of Mother Rylander. This 93 year old angel, in such an endearing and consoling way, shared with me of her struggle having lost her husband and two daughters. The death of her oldest was really hard in that even though she was raised in a Christian home, Mother Rogers was not sure if her daughter was saved. God reassured her that she had done all she could do. She said that God told her to "let your daughter go. Release her to me. We are not to feel guilty for what our children do, especially once they are grown."

As the days have gone by I discovered that this was a problem I was having. I wanted to keep Helene here with me, but I couldn't. Even though it is so hard to do, I have to let her go. She is with the Lord. Around 6:00 p.m. I went to church for our weekly midweek Bible Study/Prayer meeting. Through God's power we were able to teach the lesson. God truly blessed the time we had together. **Emotions experienced: Denial. Depression. Exhaustion. Encouragement**.

> *The angel of the Lord encamps around those*
> *who fear him, and he delivers them.*
> *Psalm 34:7*

August 20 - Thursday

It's amazing how God works. As you may note, one symptom of grief is a lack of sleep at night. For the last week or so I had not been resting well, but last night I believe it caught up with me as I slept about 8 hours. I left the television on that night (I can smile now, because Helene would have been fussing at me for this). I was suddenly awakened at precisely 6:30 a.m. by a movie called *Over My Dead Body*. Bear with me for a moment, but the story was about a woman who died on her wedding day and was prevented from entering heaven until she performed one last good deed. The good deed was giving her fiancée (now, after one year of still grieving over her death) permission to move on with his life.

I marvel at God's awesomeness and control of all things in revealing His will for us individually. No one could tell me He does not care. In my spirit I sensed that it was God's way of confirming some things that Pastor Gabriel Lewis had shared with me and Helene's reassurance and approval to me that one day I find a new wife and companion. I cannot stress the importance of an open relationship where communication is the key. Again we talked about everything. We do know that, unlike this character in the movie, Helene is not in some purgatory waiting to enter heaven because we know that *"to be absent from the body is to be present with the Lord."* **Emotions experienced: Awe. Joy. Peace. Encouragement. Guilt. Hope.**

August 21 – Friday

Unfortunately I did not get much sleep again last night. I got up and went to work. Did not get anything accomplished. Still somewhat in a daze. I received an encouraging call from Pastor Kevin Butcher. I shared with Kevin how blessed and grateful to God I was in knowing that He had been faithful to Helene and that in that very moment when she took her last breath, God was there to receive her. I quote from James Moore author of *When Grief Breaks Your Heart*.... "He is on both sides of the grave."

Kevin expressed that his prayer for me would be that in my dying hour I see Helene as I enter the glory and presence of our Lord. That too, is my prayer. The need to see my family became overwhelming, so I took a trip up to Ypsilanti. After a brief visit, I returned home. **Emotions experienced: Grief. Encouragement. Joy. Loneliness.**

August 22 – Saturday

I received a call from Mother Rylander's son, Pastor Herbert Rylander of Hartford, Connecticut. He shared with me of the impact that Helene and I have made in the "Kingdom of God" and how important that it continue. She fought her fight, finished her course and kept the faith. I'm still fighting and still running my course. When I was feeling really low, his words to not give up or give in were very up-lifting.

Helene and I were childhood sweethearts who attended the same high school together. As an athlete, I would always look up in the stands to see my girl rooting for me. This reminded me of Hebrews 12:1 where the writer describes a cloud of witness up in heaven cheering and encouraging us on in the faith. I praise God that now Helene is among those witnesses, and I know that she's my number one fan.

Around 4:30 that afternoon I picked up an old classmate and friend, Johnny to go to a class reunion bowling event. For the first time since Helene's funeral, I had to pass the cemetery on Woodward and 12 mile where she was buried. This became a very emotional moment for me. The reality of Helene being gone was too much for me to bear. I was able to get myself together. I thank God for laughter. If there was anyone who could make Helene and me laugh, it was my friend Johnny. He sensed that I was down and said something that made me smile. I had a wonderful time being with my friends that evening. I made it a point to go to all who attended and let them know that I loved each and every one of them. As I arrived home late that night, I found it very difficult to have to come in alone. **Emotions experi-**

enced: **Encouragement. Some Sorrow. Loneliness at times. Grateful for friends.**

4

Running On Empty

August 23 - Sunday

Because I was not sure when I might return to the pulpit, I had asked one of our ministers at the church to be prepared to preach. This Sunday was our 2nd Annual Family & Friends Day. The church was full to capacity that morning. A wonderful spirit was evident. While in my study God revealed to me a word. I accepted the challenge and acknowledged the importance of relying on God's power to help at this time. I was blessed that my son Gene and his family had come down from Ypsilanti that morning. My subject was "Running on Empty," coming from I Kings 19:1-8.

It is ironic that where I was at this time of my journey is where the prophet Elijah found himself. Even though I did not experience any suicidal thoughts, I did feel like calling it a day and leaving everything behind. However, God had revealed to me that He would give me what I need to go on. As God had sent an angel to Elijah, He had been sending angels to minister to me along this journey.

After service I came home and enjoyed time with my family. **Emotions: Strength from the Presence of God within. Encouragement. Exhaustion. Joyful.**

> *Jesus said to me, "My grace is sufficient for you,*
> *for my power is made perfect in weakness."*
> *.... That is why, for Christ sake, I delight*
> *in weaknesses, in insults, in hardships,*
> *in persecutions, in difficulties.*
> *For when I am weak,*
> *then I am strong.*
> *II Corinthians 12:9-10*

August 24 – Monday

Woke up early this morning with Helene on my mind. I shared some things I was experiencing with Sister Deborah Daniels via email. Following is my letter:

Hi Sister Daniels,

I hope I'm not bothering you, but out of all the many wonderful people who have embraced me and surrounded me at this time, your letter to me seems to really sense what I'm experiencing. I have never in my life felt this way before. You are right in that silence is always best, but some just don't know that. I thank God for them nevertheless, for their intentions are noble.

Helene and I had been together since we were 14 years old. I've thought about totally wanting to give up and leave everything. God has since helped me come to myself on that. It seems like everywhere I go, we've been there and everything I see, reminds me of her. When I've thought I could not cry another tear......

I know that time will heal this pain I'm feeling....... But it feels like time has stood still be-

cause the pain is so deep. Just tonight I cried out in total disbelief that this has happened and that I must be dreaming — she's not gone. I've had moments of mixed emotions in which I've spent in total praise to God for her life and how she loved God and allowed herself to be used of Him and then turn around in so much grief.

I can not curse God, but I am upset that He decided now and not later. I must admit that it has been selfish on my part wanting her to stay. She had been sick and suffering for a long time. God is good in that He knew what was best for her, not necessarily what would keep me happy.

Our twin grandchildren were just born, and we had so many hopes and dreams of spending time with them. We've worked together in ministry for so long, it just will not be the same. I know God has a continued work for me, but to be frank.... I am used to sharing it with someone. I am grateful for the time we did have, but that does not lessen the pain.

I'm back at work so as not to be home idle. When I got home I had retired for the night, but something urged me to get up and take a ride on my motorcycle all the way to Pontiac to try to escape. Then came the reality that she is not here to meet me at the door.

I'm sorry to burden you with all this. I can now realize what you must have gone through last year with your loss. Please forgive me if

*this possibly brings up feelings for your hus-
band. I just needed to release some of this I'm
feeling to someone who has been there and has
learned to some extent what to do to cope with
the many emotional levels "when grief breaks
your heart."*

*Praise God, I was actually able to preach yes-
terday for the first time. God truly blessed as
we talked about "Running on Empty," from I
Kings 19 about Elijah under the juniper tree.
I'm having days of victory, days of despair and
sometimes great depression.   The devil is a
liar, and I know it's going to be all right.*

*How are you doing? I hope if there is anything
that I can do to help you, please do not hesitate
to let me know. Thank you for being there for
me as one who truly understands.   Look forward to hearing from the Lord through you his
vessel next month.*

*Blessings,
Pastor Farris*

As I sat, I found myself in the spirit praising
God and thanking Him for Helene and the life
she lived and how she allowed herself to be
used by Him. No sooner that I knew it, my
praise began to change to agonizing grief. I
hurt so much until I began hyperventilating.
Oh how I miss her. I somehow was able to get
myself together and go to work. I received a
number of calls from some friends (Peter, Jim
and Craig) concerned about me. **Emotions:**

Praise. Grief. Some Depression. Began to feel a cleansing take place. Experiencing God in a way I never have before.

The Lord your God is with you, he is mighty to save.
He will take great delight in you, he will quiet
you with his love, he will
rejoice over you with singing.
Zephaniah 3:17

August 25 – Tuesday

Did not get much sleep. Woke up again with Helene on my mind. Received a reply from Sister Daniels. It is as follows:

Pastor Farris,

Thank you so much for your e-mail! I bless God that you know that you could talk to me and that I would understand.

I remember driving down The Lodge and wanting to run my car into the wall. It wasn't that I wanted to die. I just wanted to FEEL! I was so numb that I just wanted to feel something. I remember being at the funeral and thinking, "Wait until I tell Eugene who I saw today."

I cannot even imagine the depths of your agony, having been with your beloved for such a long time. When I met my sweetie, he was in his 40s with a failed marriage behind him; and I was in my 30s, and had sworn off men forever. BUT GOD...

In the midst of it all, the old hymn "Count your blessings" would carry me. I will not say that this will work for you. However I would start by saying, "Number one - I had 20 years with the man God made for me. Not many people can say that, and go on from there."

I am glad that you are back in the pulpit. The week after my husband's funeral was Senior Appreciation Day at Corinthian, and I was chairperson. It was some time to think about something else besides my grief. The following week, I went back to work. It was a place where I could go, and none of the customers asked how I was "making it," or squeezing my hand. I could just say, "Thank you for shopping with us," and make light conversation. It really helped.

I wasn't really angry with God, however, I was often angry at Eugene. I could not understand why he would leave me, knowing how much I loved him. The more I opened my eyes as I began to go through all the red tape of loss, the more I realized that he knew he was going to leave me soon and did not tell me. There are days when I still fuss at him for that!

I want to pass on one thing my auntie (whose been a widow for 15 years) told me. She said, "Don't make any important decisions for a year." For at least one year, we really are almost insane. I will see you fourth Sunday in September. I am here if you need someone.

Yours in His service,
Sis. Deborah Daniels

Because Helene ministered to so many people in so many ways, her absence would truly be apparent. One such need involved a member who every morning called her. I informed this member of my availability to receive that call even though I knew I could not take Helene's place. This morning she took me up on it. Her call was not to receive but to give, for her concern was evident, very much welcomed and a tremendous blessing to me. I went to work. Had lunched with a pastor friend who shared with me that I "must go through this cleansing process as God was preparing me for greater blessings." At this time I could not imagine a greater blessing than that which I had in my wife Helene, but I have always said that God has a way of outdoing Himself. When you think it can't get any better than this, here He comes and does something greater. I received this word with great anticipation.

His advice was to take my time and let God do what He needed to do in me. Later some family members came by the house to help with the acknowledgments and to get some of Helene's things packed. I found that this would be a hard thing to do. My sister Gloria comforted me with these words – "We love you and are here to take care of you." Thank you all for continuing to be here for me. **Emotions: Depression. Encouragement. Grief.**

August 26 – Wednesday
I went to work this morning. I received a call

from Sister Waters checking how I was doing. Reflected on Helene's 50th birthday party we had on the 24th of July. Helene was so happy to have her family and friends there. I shared with Janice of going in the cabinet and seeing the candles from her cake and how it brought such sorrow and pain. We had talked about using them on my cake in January. I am asking God for strength to enable me to keep the candles, that I might be able to reflect on this time now and praise God for the victory when I celebrate my 50th birthday, if it be His will.

We began Day One of our Youth Explosion at the church. I found myself in a daze. Even though present, I really was not there. I was given a beautiful memorial gift from Tanisha, a youth member of the church. Thank you so much Tanisha. **Emotions experienced: Much Sorrow. Depression.   Joy.   Stress related to Dion's situation**.

August 27 - Thursday

I got up this morning with Helene on my mind. I saw a movie called *Sling Blade* for the first time. It was similar to one of our favorite movies called *The Apostle*. I know Helene would have enjoyed it. As I was looking at it I began to praise God for helping me to reflect on memorable times Helene and I shared. These memories caused me to become consumed with looking at pictures and remembering our life together. So much pain from within began to come out. Around 12:00 noon

I took Dion to the Social Security office to take care of some business. As we sat with representatives getting his information, tears begin to flow as I rejoiced in thinking of Helene and how we worked so hard and looked so forward to our son getting the financial resources he needed for his care.

Day Two Youth Explosion. As I had some time alone with the youth evangelist for the night who was one of Gene's high school classmates, I shared with him some things I've learned and experienced on this journey. His reply was of how he looked forward to see what God will have done with me when the process was over. Even though the service was great, it was another night I really was not there. **Emotions: Tremendous Grief. Thanksgiving. Gratitude. Depression. Numbness. Great Agony. Loneliness. Praise.**

For we know that in all things God works
for the good of those who love him,
who have been called according
to his purposes.
Romans 8:28

August 28 - Friday
I woke up to a morning not beginning well for me. Struggled with guilt that I could have done more to prevent Helene's death. I was not her "protector of the people" as she had so much depended on me being for her. I went to work but accomplished very little. Very numb. I should not have gone, but I thought I

needed to be busy. Appeared to be very moody and depressed.

Day Three Youth Explosion. Helene and I were blessed to be able to share with many young couples about marriage. I shared with the youth evangelist for the evening who unfortunately was experiencing the pain of separation with his wife due to divorce about taking time when seeking a mate for life. I was blessed by the music ministry these three days. I could feel the cleansing process beginning to happen from within. **Emotions experienced: Work related stress. Guilt. Loneliness. Joy. Encouragement. Depression. Moodiness.**

August 29 - Saturday

As I awakened this morning I said to myself "Lord am I still here," realizing with great disappointment that I was still in the land of the living, hoping that instead I might now be with my Helene in glory. I needed to see the babies, so I drove to Ypsilanti. Dari was not there. I had time to be alone with the twins. I experienced a special moment with JD and "Helene." While on my way home, I received a call from two pastor friends, Alvin Lewis and Derrick Walton. Both calls were very encouraging. Pastor Lewis's words of encouragement were "Of all the special people God used in the Bible, none of them, brother, were exempt from suffering. Be encouraged. Paul even said that it was for "his good." Know that you are not alone. We are all here with you." I arrived home around 9:30 that evening very tired. **Emotions experienced: Great Disappointment. Depression. Love. Loneliness. Encouragement.**

5

Strength Renewed

August 30 – Sunday

Woke up this morning reflecting on just how much I loved Helene, and whether I could ever love another woman as much again. I went to church. It was 5th Sunday and Youth Day. Helene would have been so proud of the children. The guest preacher, my angel that day, Reverend David Reed, preached an anointed message "How Will You Finish?" – addressing the importance of allowing the processes of life, and purposes of God in those processes to fully develop their accomplished end. The presence of the Lord's Spirit was really evident in the service. As important was how we should come before God with a broken and contrite spirit in order for God to use us. I shared a special moment with my sister Gloria. I was encouraged by a member who expressed appreciation to me of being so transparent in grieving and how it has been a "blessing to her." **Emotions experienced: Guilt. Gratefulness. Some Grief. Praise and Thanksgiving. Encouragement.**

August 31 – Monday

I got up early. Reality is now beginning to set in that Helene is gone. I went to work. Somewhat in a daze. Was OK until asked to review the mission's newsletter in which the lead story was Helene. I became depressed and grief stricken. The day began to go downhill. While in a meeting I began to question my abilities to take the mission to the next level, acknowledging that I need to be reconnected with God. God has kept a hold of me even though I had let go of His hand. "Lord help me, a sinner. I need you. Help me once again to feel your presence in my life. Help me to return to your word as I ought." I really need to get away. I needed to take focus off me, so I visited a mother in the hospital.

Came home and found in the mail a card and very personal letter from another mother of the church. I truly thank God for "our mothers." It was so wonderful and encouraging. She spoke of the impact that Helene had on her life, and I quote, "Thank God for the wonderful example of Christian love from this virtuous woman, wife, mother, sister, daughter, daughter-in-law, aunt and grandmother." It included this tract by Glenda Fulton Davis that spoke to the promises of God to help me in my sorrow:

He Gathers Every Teardrop

Regardless of the circumstance,
Regardless of the fear,
Regardless of the pain we bear,
Regardless of the tear,

Our God is ever in control,
Performing as He should,
And He has promised in His word,
To work things for our good,

But as a loving Father would,

He sometimes lets us cry,
To cleanse the hurt out of our hearts,
To wash it from our eyes,

Yet gently gathers He the tears
Within His hands to stay
Until He turns them into pearls,
And gives them back someday.

I was so very grateful. Had a long talk with Sister Waters ending in her praying for me. A neighbor and high school mate came by and blessed me with a monetary gift. What a blessing it was as we shared just about "life" and the Lord. Helene's "best friend" Randi, an 8 year old youth from the church, called as she had every day since Helene's passing to say, "Pastor, just calling to see how you're doing, bye." **Emotions experienced: Work related stress. Confusion. Loneliness. Despair. Doubt. Depression. Peace. Gratitude. Encouragement.**

My God will supply all your needs
according to his glorious
riches in glory by
Christ Jesus.
Philippians 4:19

September 1 – Tuesday

Woke up around 3:30 a.m. Had mentioned yesterday to Janice that I had not yet seen Helene in any dreams. I asked God to grant me this one request. I long to see her in some way. To hear her voice. To somehow be able to touch her and say "I love you" and for her to say back "I love you too"… if only in my dreams. I realized that I could not go to work today. Would be really of no use. I decided to visit Mother Rylander. Afterward, I met Peter Tassi, a friend and member of our mission board, for an early dinner. I shared with him how I must be able to know God's will and direction for my life. Needed to take some time off after September. With Helene gone, nothing will ever be the same. A "new norm" will have to be established. Don't know what that will look like. Only time will tell. I'm grateful to God for dispatching Peter to be available for me to talk out how I have been feeling.

This evening, I was able finally to talk with my son Dion. I sensed his hurt regarding his mother but was unable to get anything out of him. "Lord please help my son. You are the only one who can really change him, and help with his special need. I love him as I know you do." **Emotions experienced: Longing for sign of Helene communicating to me – the hurt of not being able to say goodbye. Deep Heartfelt Agony. Some healing beginning to take place. Despair concerning Dion.**

September 2 – Wednesday

I got up early in preparation of taking Dion to his appointment. I was blessed that it appeared to be a place that might work out for him. I pray for my son that God will keep him and help him. Coming from Pontiac, as I was passing Roseland Park Cemetery where Helene's grave is, I was overcome by a strong emotional urge to visit her grave. As I came upon it, the next thing that I knew, I found myself prostrate over her, weeping uncontrollably. After about 15 minutes or so, I left and stopped by the hospital to visit a friend and co-worker who had suffered a heart attack yesterday. I went to work and attempted to be busy until it was time for Bible Study at the church. God is really speaking to me about some things related to the ministry.

While searching on the internet for some additional information that would be helpful in understanding this process, I was blessed to come across an essay that expressed God's Plan For My Life. It has really spoken to my heart about how important it is for me to get closer to God right now and depend exclusively on Him for all I need. To find satisfaction in Him first, and He will give me "that perfect love" I am missing. I went to Bible Study that evening and taught from 1 Peter 5:6 -7 – "He Cares." I was able to share some things I am experiencing while on this journey. The Lord really blessed our time together. **Emotions experienced: Praise and Thanksgiving for answered prayer. Grief and Sorrow. Hope. Cleansing. Joy. Encouragement.**

September 3 – Thursday

I woke up this morning around 2:00 a.m. I praise God that this morning Dion is at a place and hopefully is on the road of restoration and deliverance. I finally was able to return to bed

around 9:30 a.m. Amazingly, once again God
granted me a sign. A movie was on by the
name of *P.S. I Love You.* - bottom line.....
Don't hold onto what was. What was then was
wonderful. Who I am now is due to what
Helene and I had. She completed me. Because of the remarkable woman that she was, I
am the man I am today. I thank God for her
however, though it is even harder to write, let
alone say, Helene is gone. She was a chapter
in my life that I will cherish for the rest of my
life. She's gone, never to return. It's O.K. to
move on. It's O.K. to live again. Thank you
Lord for showing me this. Sweetheart, I will
be fine. Went to work around 1:00 p.m. for a
special meeting. Was somewhat productive
having a lot to do in preparation for the mission's 60th anniversary next week. Leaving
the mission to run some errands, I again began
to think about Helene and unfortunately became very depressed. The rest of the day,
pretty much a daze. Today's emotional roller
coaster really brought me back to what Sister
Daniels said, that for a while we are insane. I
arrived home around 5:30 p.m. After eating
dinner that my mom had cooked for me, I went
to bed around 6:45 p.m.. **Emotions experienced: Gratitude. Confidence in the future.
Confused. Hope. Peace. Depression. Fatigue.**

September 4 – Friday
Woke up around 3:30 a.m. feeling very rested.
The house had begun to get a bit out of order,
so I cleaned up and washed some clothes.

Looked forward to picking up Dari tomorrow to take her to the State Fair. I'm feeling really good this morning. For the first time in about four weeks, I had some personal time with the Lord in devotion. I received a wonderfully uplifting email from my angel Sister Edna that included a "Lesson from the Eagle" that really put some things in perspective about the importance of perseverance.

Eagles enjoy the longest life expectancy among bird species. They can live up to 70 years. In order to survive, they have to make a critical decision at the age of 40. When eagles turn 40, their claws are weakened, and it is hard for them to catch prey. Their beaks are growing long and almost touching their chest. Their wings are heavier due to thick and long feathers.

They have 2 options, to die or to undergo a painful transformation. They decide to undergo the painful transformation. They fly to mountain tops to build their home and rest. This is the beginning of 150 days of perseverance and a steadfast journey! They have to hit their beaks against the rock till they fall off. Then they must wait patiently for their new beaks to grow. They will use their new beaks to pull out their nails. With their newly grown nails, they will then clean off their old feathers. Five months later, the eagles will fly again with new feathers and renewed strength for another thirty years.

Sometimes we have to make difficult decisions in life to embark on a new journey. We have to let go of old habits and traditions and let ourselves fly and soar like the eagle.

> *But they that wait upon the Lord shall*
> *renew their strength;*
> *they shall mount up with wings as eagles;*
> *they shall run, and not be weary;*
> *they shall walk and not faint.*
> *Isaiah 40:31*

If we put down our old-self, eagerly pick up new skills, we are able to explore the undiscovered talents in us!

For me, this was the beginning of my way out of this valley of despair. I got myself together and went to work. While on my way, God revealed to me that He knew how much I loved Helene, but He challenged me to examine my love for Him. It put into my mind the question Jesus asked Peter in John 21:15… "loveth thou me more than these?" The pain you are feeling right now with your wife gone, is it the same pain you feel when you have sinned against me? Does it hurt as bad when you find your walk with me is not as it should be? When I tell you to do something and you don't do it, are you in agony as you were just the other day? God, through this process is helping me to see that nothing and no one should be closer than Himself. Now I know this (intellectually), but it's ironic that God has to take us to certain places in order for us to get it in our heart that we see Him more clearly.

I arrived at work and got a lot accomplished. Took a break for a moment and went out for lunch with a new friend, Roger, who was concerned about how I was doing. Shared with him some things God was doing in my life. Roger presented me with a devotional book entitled "My Utmost for His Highest" by Oswald Chambers. After lunch I looked at the message for this day, and amazingly it referenced Luke 14:26 and how Jesus said that He would not be second to any other relationships (father, mother, "wife" or children) in order for us to be His disciples. This was a hard pill to swallow, and as some would say... *it was tight, but it was right.*

As I reflected on our marriage and what made it so wonderful and fulfilling, I discovered that it was not that either of us loved the other more than God, but because we loved God so, we had that perfect love for each other. I stated in the beginning that I believe there is no relationship that comes close to that which Christ has for His church than that of a husband and wife. Where I am now that my "Clair" (Helene) is gone is that my relationship with God must grow deeper. Until I am satisfied with "HIM" and exclusive to "HIM", I will not be able to experience again anything close to what Helene and I had in "HIM." **Emotions experienced: Hope. Conviction. Encouragement. Enlightenment.**

6

A Long Road Ahead

September 5 – Saturday

Woke up this morning around 3:45 a.m. It is one month to the day that Helene made her transition from labor to reward. "God, I know that I did not bring myself to this point." As I looked back at where I was and where I am now, all I can do is thank God for the strength and for the many who have helped me this far. I now look so forward to waking up each morning in such anticipation of what God is going to do. To start this day, I received this from my friend Pastor Gabe.

ABUNDANT INCREASE OF FAVOR
And I will make of you a great nation,
and I will bless you
[with abundant increase of favors]
and make your name famous and distinguished,
and you will be a blessing
[dispensing good to others]"
(Genesis 12:2 (AMP)).

I picked up my granddaughter Dari and went to the State Fair with my mom and sister Cecilia. We had a great time together, however, I did experience a moment of sadness seeing Dari enjoy the rides but Helene was not here with us. When we arrived home for the evening, Dari really felt Helene's absence and how lonely "we" now were. She called her mommy almost in tears asking her to come spend the

night with us. I shared with her how grateful I
was to her for being with me this weekend because I understood how she was feeling and
how lonely "we" were. We cried for a moment
together until she, as children do, had the
greatest solution to the problem. *"Grandpa
you need to get a dog and a cat so you won't
be alone and you will have someone to talk
to."* Kids can say the darnedest things. I told
her "Grandma and I had thought about getting
a dog, but we don't do cats." I was blessed
today, for I had with me my Dari. Unlike a
month ago, again the sun shined, but it was not
a dark day. **Emotions experienced: Victory.
Joy. Hope. Encouragement. A Little Sadness. Fatigue.**

September 6 – Sunday

It was a very interesting morning to wake up
with a 5 year old and having to get her up myself, get her dressed and fed before going to
church. I know that for you mothers, it's no
big thing, it's just what you do. Please pray for
me, for I will have the addition of my two twin
grand babies soon. That will really be interesting. Lord, know, I will really miss Helene
then.

Once we arrived at church, being the first Sunday of the month and the busiest, we were
blessed to have two girls as candidates for bap-
tism. So much did I depend on Helene in ministry that I found myself in tears after baptiz-
ing, due to the fact that she always met me in

the choir room to assist me in changing my wet clothes, but of course she was not there. I shared with the congregation in my sermon, on a personal note, some things that God was dealing with me. My subject was from John 21:15- "Do you love me?" After services were over, one of our members, 5 year old Emanuel wanted to give me a picture that he made. It was a picture of Helene in heaven smiling and a picture of me here on earth in tears. Thank you "Manny." Even though you may not see it, my tears are tears of joy just knowing that Sister Farris is smiling because she is with Jesus.

But I would not have you to be ignorant, brethren, con-cerning them which are asleep, that ye sorrow not, even as others which have no hope.
I Thessalonians 4:13

Family members came by the house after church. When asked how I was doing, I shared with some how I have embraced the process. God gave us people to love, and knowing that death will come to those we love, God's purpose for grief is designed to make us better. He will do this for us if we allow Him to. Look at all the people in your life who are no longer with you. Your still being able to stand is a tribute to the faithfulness of God to keep you from falling. **Emotions experienced: Brief Grief. Gratitude. Praise. Peace. Joy. Encouragement.**

September 7—Monday
Today is Labor Day, the first holiday in more

than 35 years that Helene and I were not together. I did not do much today. Went down to
the mission for a while, to my sister Deborah's
house and then came home. I really felt nothing today. I had many invitations to come and
have dinner but really wanted to be alone. I
missed my wife. **Emotions experienced:
Numb. Very lonely.**

September 8– Tuesday

I got up pretty early this morning. Had devotion, feeling pretty good, and believe it or not,
very rested. Began organizing my day due to
the fact that I had a lot I needed to get accomplished because of the mission's upcoming
event in 5 days. I went to work. Should have
stayed home, not because of my personal life
but because of Satan being busy trying to sabotage some things we as staff needed to get
done. We worked through the problems by not
stressing out on matters that were out of our
control. After coming home late that afternoon, I received a call from Pastor Gabe.
Again he was of great encouragement. When I
first began this journal, its intent was primarily
to help me deal with my pain. It was a way for
me to systematically monitor what God was
doing, seeing that I was so much in the valley
of darkness and sorrow. I wanted to be able to
look back and see chronologically from where
He had brought me.

As a man and then pastor, I know that we can
constantly be in a state of denial concerning

our feelings and pain. Because of the tremendous pressure and responsibility we have to the people we serve and to God, we often suppress our true feelings of the heart.

Many might feel that they do not have the right to acknowledge "I hurt, God I'm mad, I don't care" because of possibly thinking God will get up set. We are not "superman." We cannot run faster than a locomotive. We do not leap tall buildings with a single bound. We are simply earthen vessels chosen by God to carry this message of hope in His son Jesus Christ. I believe that some, if not all, of what I am sharing with you is what scores of others feel, but at times are too proud to share or too stubborn to acknowledge. This is one reason I believe God has now taken over the writing of this journey. His purpose is to help me see Him more clearly and to use my experience helping others come to grip with their inner emotions and feelings of pain. Moreover, to discover that He understands and is there to help them. **Emotions experienced: Gratitude for God's revealed grace. Encouragement. Fulfillment of purpose.**

September 9—Wednesday
I had a somewhat restless night. As I got up, I attempted to get my daily devotional book, a cup of coffee, and set down for some time with the Lord, but instead, I picked up one of the picture albums I had recently made of Helene. This, no doubt, began a day of ex-

treme depression and sorrow. As I looked at them, tears began to flow. I never was able to get back to read my devotional this morning.

As this journey continues, I am coming to face my true feelings. So often we are not truthful to ourselves and others when we need to be. When not feeling good, we'll say "I'm all right," when asked. We need to face the fact that our body language, countenance, and even our voice will give us away. While at work, as much as I tried to be productive and get things done, it showed that I was hurting. I got a phone call from a member of the church who, I believe before I could say anything, sensed something was wrong. I was blessed not too long after that member appeared in my office and prayed for me.

Tonight is our scheduled Bible Study/Prayer meeting at the church; however, I really didn't feel like even going, and you know, that's all right. It's all right sometimes to say, "I need some time just for me." I thank God for our preachers at the church. I was able to call them both and ask them to carry on.

Never say what you will not do. I once wondered why people went to the cemetery to visit their loved ones so much. After all, we know that "they are not there." I must now apologize to all who find it necessary to go for as long as they wish and as often as it takes, for this is their way of coping and their "journey."

I visited Helene's grave site again today. I took with me some devotional material, sat down on the ground beside her and began to read. Once I was done, I just praised God for who He is and Helene for who she was. I talked to her about some things God was doing with me, and about how excited I was writing this book. We had many times thought about writing a book together, having experienced so much. I smiled when I thought to myself that if she could, she would tell me some really exciting things about God firsthand. I've often wondered what it's really like, once you make that transition. Certainly not as portrayed in the movies.

> *But as it is written, Eye hath not see, nor ear heard,*
> *Neither have entered into the heart of man,*
> *The things which God hath prepared*
> *for them that love Him.*
> *1 Corinthians 2:9*

This had to be the most beautiful and pleasant day of the entire year. As I sat under the sun, I laid down on the ground next to her grave. As you know, I've had so many restless nights tossing and turning because I've missed my wife lying next to me in bed. As insane as it might sound, I actually imagined that Helene was right there with me.

Such peace and tranquility overcame me until I actually fell asleep. An hour must have gone by. As I woke up my focus was drawn to a blade of grass. On the blade was an ant going up and down the blade. This brought to my

mind how wonderful God is to me. As confused and sinful as I am, God still cares. At
times I've doubted Him, but He has still been
faithful.

God said to me, "You see this ant, he has nothing to worry about. All he will need I will provide for him. All you need, even more so I
will provide for you. You're gonna make it."
This day having started out as it had, I was so
blessed and encouraged when God made a way
for me to take some time "our special time together" - me, my Clair, an ant, and God, in a
not too distant place, on a bright and sunny
day. **Emotions experienced: Gratitude. Re-
leased Guilt. Better understanding of what
others feel because of having experienced it
to the same level or degree). Grief. Loneliness. Depression. Hope. Peace. Joy.**

September 10—Thursday

This journey over the last month has been very
interesting in that God has done things so
"outside the box." This morning I was awakened by a long distant phone call around 5:52
a.m. from Augusta, Georgia. The caller was
someone who I had met only once. She first
made sure that it was me and then began to
scream (I mean, sing) this song I never heard
before. She was very encouraging, ensuring
me that God cared and "had my back", then
she prayed for me. With all my heart I thank
God for her and her sincere words of condo-
lence and encouragement. Once I arrived at

work, a brother at the mission came into my office and asked if he could have a word of prayer with me. I left work early, having to run some errands. Received a call from my sister to come down and get something to eat. **Emotions experienced: Fatigue. Encouragement.**

September 11—Friday

Woke up this morning at precisely 2:30 a.m., having slept for 3 to 4 hours at the most. It's one day left before the event, and it seems like hundreds of things need to be done. Clearly, I am feeling an enormous amount of pressure and stress. I received a call from my friend, Craig, to see if we could meet for coffee. Neither one of us could meet for long, only 5 minutes. I have a tremendous support system of family and friends who love me and to whom I'm grateful. I shared with Craig how down and depressed I was feeling, and whether I had what it takes to continue at the mission. Craig's reply was that it was natural, since I have just experienced half of myself taken away in Helene. He offered prayer, and I took this opportunity to cry. Thank you Craig. I hurried to work in the midst of a flow of tears. So much pain! Once there I realized there was much work to be done and I thought I would be all right as long as I stayed busy with my mind on something else, but the day would prove me wrong.

As details began to be worked out, I sat down

to get a bite to eat. As people came in and out of the office I found myself crying again. I did not want to bring attention to myself, so I hurried and finished my lunch. As the day went on I felt very moody and at times short fused. On my list of things that I was responsible for was making sure that we met all the city guidelines for the event in terms of providing food to the public. Helene had received the training and certification in this area and would naturally have handled all these details effortlessly. So much did I depend on her. This evening my church, Open Door Gospel Tabernacle, and our dear friends from Ward Presbyterian Church joined for a wonderful fellowship in serving the clients at the mission called "Second Friday."

We look forward every month coming together. I have now developed lifelong relationships because of this fellowship. One reason was because of the good food Ward would prepare but especially the "sherbet ice cream" they traditionally would serve for dessert. For Helene, this was what topped the day off. As I sat down to eat, memories of her sitting and enjoying her second bowl overcame me, and again I find myself in tears. Ward Church, don't stop bringing the sherbet ice cream. It will always be one of those special memories we can all share and remember. I finally got home late tonight. I ate my dinner and went to bed very tired and emotionally depleted. **Emotions experienced: Fatigue. Depression.**

**Much grief and sorrow. Anxiety. Moodiness.
Job related stress. Inadequacy. Loneliness.**

September 12—Saturday

Today the Open Door Rescue Mission will celebrate 60 years of service to the community. I woke up this morning with much anticipation of the day's events. So many people have worked so hard for its success. I had not been able to do much since Helene's passing and am so grateful to those who made sure that everything was taken care of. I was asked by my sister, Cecilia, whether I questioned why God would take Helene and would I have wished for her to still be suffering as she had here. I loved my wife and miss her dearly; however, I would not want her to suffer. God loved her more and did what He felt was best for her. I arrived at the mission to finish last minute details, still a little tired.

As people began to arrive I found myself beginning to get depressed. I tried to hide it by appearing busy, but it began to weigh heavily on my heart that Helene should be here to share in this celebration. Not wanting to break down in front of anyone, I ran to my office, tears flowing down my face. So much pain! I had hoped I would be able to refrain from such emotion at this time, but I just could not help it.

Some of my staff that were in the office saw me as I entered and knew something was wrong. They closed the doors, not allowing anyone to disturb me and gave me comfort. I finally got it together and went back out to greet our guests.

As the day went on, the crowd began to get larger. Many came to me and expressed their condolences for my loss. A very touching moment of silence and tribute was given in honor of Helene. The day ended with me picking up my twins from my niece Danielle's house.

As I held my granddaughter, Gabriella, in my arms and looked at her beautiful face, I thanked the Lord for this day. I believe that I eventually fell asleep around 9:30 p.m. **Emotions experienced: Anxiety. Depression. Fatigue. Joy.**

September 13—Sunday

It's 12:30 a.m., and yes, I am wide awake after approximately 3 hours of sleep. I might need to consider the suggestion of taking something that will help me to sleep. I thought that now with the celebration behind me I would feel some relief of pressure from within, but this morning it hasn't. There is a saying that God will put on us only what we are able to bear. Right now, as I am writing these words, what I am feeling is unbearable. My heart is hurting, and the pain is indescribable.

> *My heart is sore pained within me:*
> *and the terrors of death*
> *are fallen upon me. Fearfulness and trembling*
> *are come upon me, and horror hath overwhelmed me.*
> *And I said, Oh that I had wings*
> *like a dove! For then*

would I fly away
and be at rest.
Psalm 55:5-6

I have made the analogy when counseling couples that the wonderful thing about their union will be whatever number of burdens each may bring to the relationship, they all will be cut in half, being shared with your spouse.

Helene and I shared everything. She asked me several years ago, when I became pastor of the church and director of a separate ministry whether I could do both effectively, keeping in mind my primary responsibilities as a husband and father. At that time I said yes confidently. One reason that I was able to say it was because I had her with me. Whatever challenges or opportunities I faced, she was there to face them with me. They were not my problems but "our" problems. She was the epitome of what a true helpmeet is to be. Where I was weak or lacking, her strength would make up the difference. Now that she's gone, a part of me is gone. What do I do now?

These thoughts of inadequacy brought to mind how Moses felt when commissioned by God to go tell Pharaoh to let my people go, and God said to him parenthetically it will not be by your strength that you will go.

God was saying to me, "It will not be by Helene that you will stand." You will stand because of who "I AM."

Not by power nor my might
by my spirit saith the Lord.
Zechariah 4:6

I shared with you a couple of days ago about the importance of getting real and being honest with your feelings. I must confess that I am very vulnerable at this time. I loved my wife, was faithful to her all our years together, but now feelings for the need of companionship are very strong. Please pray with me and for me that God will give me the strength not to give into the temptations of the flesh that would have me to sin.

Pull me out of the net that they have laid privily for me:
for thou art my strength.
Psalm 31:4

There hath no temptation taken you but such as is
common to man:
but God is faithful, who will not suffer you
to be tempted above that ye are able;
but will with the temptation
also make a way of escape that ye
may be able to bear it.
1 Corinthians 10:13

It is now about 8:30 a.m. I went to church this morning. It was Seniors Day at our church, our annual day of recognition to all the elderly. Our guest preacher, Reverend Huey Taylor, truly became a godsend and my angel this day. He shared with me words of encouragement as one who understands. It was just 2 years ago that his wife of 54 years passed right in his arms. What has helped him thus far has been a mission focused on allowing God to work on him. More than anything, he said, was that I needed to know that Helene's wish for me would be that I go higher in the blessings of God and not settle or become dormant grieving for her. Because she is in heaven concerned about me here, God will allow her to personally (I don't know how or when) relieve me of the anguish I am at times feeling. His sermon was as inspiring, coming from Exodus 14: 11-15 — "I've Come Too Far To Turn Around." We had a glorious time of praise and worship.

Afterward, I enjoyed the time with my grand babies, even though it proved too much for me alone, with them being just 2 months old. I had to call my niece, Danielle, to help me with them. I retired for the night hoping to now be able to get some sleep. **Emotions experienced: Fatigue. Confusion. Praise and Worship. Lack of Confidence. Guilt. Loneliness. Encouragement. Joy.**

September 14—Monday

I woke up around 6:00 a.m. refreshed. I prayed, asking the Lord to help in addressing the many issues I'm now dealing with relating to work and personal matters. I am presently in a state of complete brokenness. My reliance upon God has never been this intense and personal. A favorite hymn came to mind: "I Surrender All."

All to Jesus I surrender, All to Him I freely give;
I will ever love and trust Him, In His presence daily live.
I surrender all, I surrender all
All to Thee, my blessed Savior, I surrender all.

I truly believe that Satan is aware when God is about to bless and deliver his child. He will come with all he has to try and deter the mind of the believer what God has said concerning His promises. When you look at Jesus and His march toward Calvary, the closer that He got to the cross, the more intensified the attack against Him became. I feel in my spirit that God is about to do something huge in my life, and Satan knows it. I am being attacked on every side (can't tell it all), but Satan is a liar.

> *Greater is he that is in you,*
> *than he that is in the world.*
> *1 John 4:4*

While at work I received a call from another good friend who serves on the board of the mission offering me an invitation, if needed, to a professional grief counseling group that was beginning to meet at his church. One key to being able to handle grief is being able to share what you are feeling with someone else. I highly recommend professional help to those who need it, especially if you do not have a support system of family and friends. I am tremendously blessed and fortunate that I have such a system of support. More than that, God is dealing with me by capturing my feelings and emotions and showing me His work through people and circumstances. This may not be for everyone, but for me, it has helped me more than I believe anything ever could. Thank you to a special friend for caring.

One of my staff received an invitation for me to a dinner and bible conference from a partnering church. It was a good opportunity to network as well as not having to go home to an empty house so soon. I really enjoyed the fellowship but found out just how tired I was; I had to leave after intermission. I arrived home that evening around 8:45. I fell asleep around 9:30. **Emotions experienced: Confusion. Helplessness. Encouragement.**

September 15—Tuesday

I found myself awake around 2:30 a.m. I felt the urge to clean the house. As I have found myself doing frequently, I looked through Helene's picture album. Looking at them, I remembered the details and stories behind each one. I began to praise God for the life we had together. I'm coming to a point now of focusing more on what we shared together than what I do not have now that she is gone. For me this was major. (WOW!) I went back to bed and slept another 4 hours.

I needed to take care of some business at Social Security this morning, so I got myself together and went to the local office. Once I arrived, I found out some information that upset me greatly. It upset me because it became the result of "doing the right thing." Helene received disability benefits due to her illness. A few days after her death I reported it to Social Security. I know that some probably would not have done that so quickly, especially how hard times are right now.   At least a few months would have had to go by before reporting it. I do not say this to appear to be so good and holy (if you only knew what I know and God knows about me), just that I did not want to get caught up having to pay the money back later.   A payment that I was entitled to was stopped. Now I come to find out that the process to file a special grievance will take at lease 3 months. This is what sent me into orbit. I had to immediately ask the Lord for forgiveness.

I met a friend after work, came home around 7:00 p.m., and ate a dinner prepared by a church member. You know angels work late, too. I received a wonderful and uplifting call this evening from Pastor Jerome Williams, a former board member and dear brother in the Lord. Every Wednesday morning, Pastor Williams teaches a bible study class at the mission for staff and residences. He called just to encourage me in the Lord and stated how he will truly miss Helene's participation and enthusiasm. She really loved that class. **Emotions experienced: WOW! Anger. Remorse for ungodly behavior. Forgiveness. Peace. Encouragement.**

September 16—Wednesday
Bless the Lord, O my soul:
and all that is within me, bless his holy name.
Psalm 103:1

This morning I woke up, rested with praise and thanksgiving in my mouth. No one but the

Lord and me. All I could say was THANK YOU, THANK YOU, THANK YOU to God for my life, my wife and now the beginning of understanding His purpose for my pain. With tears flowing, I found myself in a spirit of total praise to God because of all He is proving Himself to be to me. No one can tell me that God is not a heart fixer, and that He cannot mend broken hearts.

I went to work early in order to prepare for a mission board meeting. From work I went to the mid week bible study/prayer meeting. I taught a lesson tonight from the subject " How To Get What You Want From God" coming from one of our favorite scriptures Psalm 37:4-8. In order that we obtain the desires of our hearts (wants), we must delight (gain pleasure, satisfaction and happiness) in the Lord. One of the reasons Helene and I loved this scripture so was because it became the trademark of God's favor in our lives. We were able to do so many things together that we loved doing that we should not have been able to do. We never had much by way of possessions or finances but were able to enjoy life together and to its fullest while we had it.

> *Live joyfully with the wife whom thou lovest*
> *all the days of the life of thy vanity,*
> *which he hath given thee under the sun,*
> *all the days of thy vanity;*
> *for that is thy portion in this life,*
> *and in thy labour which thou*
> *takest under the sun.....*
> *Ecclesiastes 9: 9*

The main reason I believe this was possible was because we were satisfied in Jesus. We delighted ourselves in Him. We were content in whatever He had for us, and because of that contentment, He blessed us with more ..."*above that which we asked or imagined.*"

I opened up the bible study class discussion stating that I needed God to do some specific things for me. Desires are not to be seen as something bad if there is an understanding of God and how He works. A person who has the right desires will have a growing relationship with the Lord. Since you are coming to understand His will through His Word, you will not desire anything that would not bring Him glory. In other words, your desire will not be self-centered but God-centered. To have a growing relationship with God is to be committed in all your ways to God. I welcome God to examine my desires and my plans. To alter what does not fix His purpose. To trust Him with all my heart. I believe that in doing this God will not withhold any good thing from me.

> *He that spared not his own Son, but delivered him*
> *up for us all, how shall he not with him*
> *also freely give us all things?*
> *Romans 8:32*

I was blessed in that I "belonged" completely, thoroughly and exclusively to another, my wife Helene. Because she is now gone does not mean that desire for me to "belong" is gone;

however, God has spoken to me through this following essay by an unknown author:

"No, not until you're satisfied, fulfilled and content with being loved by me <u>alone</u>; with giving yourself totally and unreservedly to me <u>alone</u>; to having an intensely personal relationship with me <u>alone</u>; discovering that only in me is your satisfaction to be planned for you.

You will never be united with another until you are united with me — exclusive of anyone or anything else, exclusive of any other desires or longings. I want you to stop planning, stop wishing, and allow me to give you the most thrilling plan existing, one that you cannot imagine. I want you to have the best. Please allow me to bring it to you. You just keep watching me, expecting great things. Keep experiencing the satisfaction that I AM. Keep listening to and learning the things I tell you. You just wait ... that's all.

Don't be anxious; don't worry. Don't look around at the things that others have or that I have given them. Don't look at the things you think you want. You just keep looking off and away up to me, or you'll miss what I want to show you. And then, when you're ready, I'll surprise you with a love far more wonderful than any you would ever have dreamed. Keep your eyes on me.

You see, while I'm working on you, I'm also

working on someone for you. When you are both satisfied and exclusively with me, and the life I have prepared for you, then you will be ready for each other and able to experience the love that exemplifies your relationship with me, and thus the perfect love."

Unknown Author

Needless to say when I read this, I was excited about the future. I know what a wonderfully blessed life I had with my wife Helene, but to know that God has a plan to give me even more than I had is mind-blowing. I've got to rest in Him. I've got to wait patiently on Him. He knows what He is doing. God wants the best for all of us. Don't settle for anything less.

*But seek ye first the kingdom of God,
and his righteousness; and all
these things shall be
added unto you.
Matthew 6:33*

7

No Pain No Gain

"Tis better to have loved and lost
than never to have loved at all."
... Poet Alfred Tennyson

A few weeks have passed in which I am no longer writing a day-to-day account of this journey. God has been working in me, speaking to me, and it appears now wants to do something different with me.

I decided to take the advice of a friend and get away for awhile. As I may have mentioned previously, Helene and I were blessed to do a lot of things because of God's grace upon us. One of those things was to enjoy yearly vacations abroad. On this particular day as I was browsing through a vacation planner book, suddenly tears began to fall. I felt such anger as never before towards God. I was definitely now venturing into unfamiliar waters, for never have I been mad at God for anything He has done. I've been greatly disappointed at times when He would not grant me what I thought I should have. However, this time I was so angry at the point I yelled at Him, "God, how dare you. I'm here planning a time away, and Helene should be here with me." I was just short of cursing God, even though I am not known to be a person who speaks profanity, but honestly, a word or two did come to mind. Don't be surprised, I do know some and so do you.

In this moment of madness, I immediately found myself in the shoes of Job when he desired a face to face with God to question why he was suffering.

> *Oh that I knew where I might find him!*
> *That I might order my cause before him,*
> *and fill my mouth with arguments.*
> *Job 23: 3-4*

I do realize, that my arms are too short to box with God, and that me being angry at Him in no way "rocked His world" or caused Him to cease from being God. I immediately came to myself humbly acknowledging my sinfulness and insignificance in comparison to His holiness. I asked Him to forgive me, and of course, He did.

> *If we confess our sins, he is faithful and just to*
> *forgive us our sins, and cleanse*
> *from all unrighteousness.*
> *1 John 1: 9*

I'm learning through all of this how better equipped I will be in understanding people. Not too many people can relate to the things Job experienced, but one thing I can say in this instance is, Brother Job, "I feel you." It's amazing how God works. To my fellow clergy and all who believe God's calling on their lives to help the hurting, God is in need of those who can relate to the hurt people are going through. We cannot talk about something that we know nothing about. Time out for the watered down, surface, feel good type of ministry that does not get to the heart of one's real need. Time out for the clichés and platitudes used to stir up emotional responses. People are hurting, and they need people who care and understand their hurt.

Let's stop making others think that everything is always all right when at times it is very much wrong. Be honest not only about the things of God but also about ourselves and the pain we personally experience. People need to see some transparency at times to know that we also hurt and are in need of God. The church is a hospital where "sin-sick" folk come to get healing. We are all sick and we all need healing.

That healing can come, even though you might not get that promotion. That healing can come, even if you are diagnosed with cancer. That healing can come, even if you lose your job. That healing is available to all who would come before God. The reason it is available is because of the sacrifice made by God.

But he was wounded for our transgressions, he was bruised
for our iniquities: the chastisement of our peace
was upon him; and with his strips
we are healed.
Isaiah 53:5

A question came to mind of what was most painful to Jesus while on Calvary. Was it the physical pain of torture and being nailed to the cross or the spiritual presence of sin being placed on Himself? Knowing how painful it is for me when I stub my toe or have a tooth ache, I cannot imagine the pain Jesus physically felt. However, to be separated from God the Father because of sin, had to be worse.

That pain was something that He had to experience

in order to fulfill His purpose for coming into the world. That pain was something He had to experience in order to fulfill the requirements of His Father. That pain was something He had to go through that mankind might be reunited with God. That pain He had to endure in order for the debt of sin to be paid.

And almost all things are by the law purged with blood;
and without the shedding of blood
there is no remission of sin.
Hebrews 9:22

We naturally do not like pain, but pain has a "purpose." Someone once said that "If I didn't have problems, I wouldn't know that God can solve them." The same can be said about pain. If I never experienced it, I would not know that God is right there to help me, comfort me and heal me. This reassurance in God's faithfulness always results in His children drawing closer to Him.

Let me again remind you that God has a plan for all of us and to get us where He wants us, we will have to go through some valleys in life. We will have to experience some turbulence, stormy weather, and dark days.

I'm discovering that when it comes to pain, it has no face on it, for it comes in many shapes and sizes. When we talk about pain, what normally comes to mind is of a physical nature, but what we need to understand is that pain can be experienced in an emotional (from your heart) and psychological (in your mind) way.

My pain of course was the loss of Helene. This

loss has touched every area of my being. Physically, I will no longer be able to touch her face, hold her hand or feel her embrace. Emotionally, I will miss that reassuring confidence that we are both in this thing together. Spiritually, we were one with God and in Christ, bone of my bone and flesh of my flesh.

Pain can come when confidence and trust in a marriage is broken through infidelity. Pain can come when one's motives are misunderstood and pride or guilt is the determining factor in the outcome of a situation. Pain can come when an addiction is the cause of you being separated from your family. Pain can come when the one you believed in lets you down. Unlike simple disappointment, this pain will occur based upon the level of intimacy and dependency one had in the other person. Pain can come when you find yourself on top of the world one minute, and in the pit of despair the next. You've been cruising on all cylinders. Life is good. Financially, bills are being paid, health wise — your last checkup was good, ministry flourishing — souls being saved and lives changed. Then, suddenly the bottom drops out. You've lost your job, bills overdue, house is up for foreclosure, loved one has been diagnosed with an incurable disease, and a scandal has hit the ministry.

Pain can bring about new opportunities and give "birth" to untapped potential. A mother giving birth to a child is no doubt in great pain; however, once the child is born, the pain is replaced with great joy because of this new life and the future possibilities and hope it will bring.

There exists on any given bush or tree, branches that are no longer producing fruit. It robs or prevents other branches from receiving the necessary nutrients it needs to be "fruitful." Branches that are producing no fruit are cut down completely. Branches that produce some fruit are pruned that they may produce more fruit. Any cutting or pruning of something will be "painful." Sometimes God has to take from that tree those "dead" branches.

I AM the true vine, and my Father is the husbandman.
Every branch in me that beareth not fruit he taketh away;
and every branch that beareth fruit, he purgeth it,
that it may bring forth more fruit.
John 15: 1-2

A rose bush really flourishes and peaks to its ultimate beauty and potential only after it has gone periodically through a pruning process. Don't resist what God is doing through your "pruning process." Don't fight against the prick of God's purpose for your life. Examine what He is trying to say to you about "you." Trust and lean on Him for the strength to endure and prevail through the pain. Even though He may choose not to reveal His purpose to us, know that it will ultimately produce a flower that will smell like a rose in the nostril of God.

That the trail of your faith, being much more precious
than of gold that perisheth, though it be tried with fire,
might be found unto praise and honour and
glory at the appearing of Jesus Christ.
1 Peter 1:7

8

Lest I Forget

We had a family tradition that was carried down from Helene's parents — Sunday mornings gathering for breakfast, thanking God for His provisions, and reciting the Lord's Prayer. I can see momma at the head of the table ending her prayer **"When I've done all I can do, receive me somewhere in thy kingdom, Amen."** Helene and I continued this tradition even after our boys were gone and out on their own. Recently, however, this has been really difficult for me. Every Sunday morning I sat at our table alone, often in tears. As I prayed to God, I thanked Him for His provisions to me and began to recite the Lord's Prayer. Even though physically I feel so alone, I know God is there with me. Needless to say, at this time, Sunday morning breakfast really doesn't have the same meaning as it once did. Oh how I miss my wife's homemade biscuits and tomato gravy.

One of the byproducts of pain is a temptation to want to just give up. We can be tempted to indulge in sin, but understand that we can also be tempted to give up on God. For about three weeks now God has strengthened me to be able to minister to others at the church. As previously mentioned, it was so important that my faith be witnessed to others.

I was blessed to be invited to bring a word to a

church we are in fellowship with for their Annual Men's Day. At the same time, our church was having its Annual Women's Day service in which Helene took very seriously overseeing and making sure was a success. This year of course, would be very special in that a special honor would be given in memory of her. Of course I had to be there.

I found myself now fixed between two opinions: to support my own church, or go and preach the gospel. I believe and teach that charity begins first at home. I knew the importance of supporting our women on their day, but I also take my calling to preach the gospel seriously. Helene would have wanted me to go and preach.

I stayed at our services for as long as I could before leaving for the other church. What I was blessed to witness of the service was wonderful. I found myself both rejoicing in the Lord and the evidence of Helene's fruit coming to fruition through the women of God she had mentored, but then tremendous grief during the lighting of the candles in her memory. Members and friends were there to console me, but time was running out, so I had to get myself together and leave for the other service. As I was leaving, I was asked whether I would be able to preach, and my reply was, "No, but the Holy Ghost is able." Before me was another opportunity for God to "show Himself mighty", and if anything would happen, God would have to do it, for I found myself again humbly "running on empty." By God's power I was able to preach. All glory and praise to Him alone.

Our message was "It's Just In Me" coming from Jeremiah 20: 7-9.

Dad (Pastor Robert Ware), a spiritual father and mentor, had shared with me recently his experience when his first wife died many years ago and how while living in Akron, Ohio, he brought her home for the funeral and had to immediately return to Akron to preach that Sunday morning. His pastor's words were "I know you're hurting, but the people need a word from you." This reminded me of how blessed I am of having this time to embrace the process with the great support of family and friends, and how the Prophet Ezekiel was unable to after his wife died, but was told by God to immediately get up and go prophesy (Ezekiel 24: 15-18).

We have a natural inclination to focus on ourselves when a crisis hits our world. This is a response of which I am guilty, and I believe God understands. However, what God has shown me through the writing of this book is, Jerome, it's not just about you. What you thought was exclusively for your healing must be used to help others also. ***My son knew no sin but became sin for you***. Lest we forget that Jesus.....

Who, being in the form of God, thought it not robbery to be equal with God: But made himself of no reputation, and took upon himself the form of a servant, and was made in the likeness of men: And being found in the fashion as a man, he humbled himself, and became obedient unto death, even the death

of the cross.
Philippians 2: 6-8

This life we have is not ours. This light that shines abroad in our hearts is not ours. Those whom God places in our lives to love are not ours to keep. It all belongs to Him. "The Lord giveth, and the Lord taketh away, blessed be the name of the Lord." Our time here is but for a moment. While we sojourn, let us always remember that it's not about us, but it's first about <u>J</u>esus, <u>o</u>thers, and then <u>y</u>ourself. Real <u>joy</u> is the realization that if you focus on serving and helping others, God will not forget you, especially in your greatest time of need.

The Son of Man did not come to be served, but to serve.
Mark 10:45

9

Handkerchief Anyone?

I would like to look at a subject that was briefly mentioned earlier of an encouraging tract that was given to me by one of the mothers of our church entitled "He Gathers Every Teardrop," by Glenda Fulton Davis. I am not ashamed to say that there exists a sensitive side of me that is prone to expressing itself through tears. During this journey, I believe I have shed enough tears to fill a five gallon container. It seems like the slightest thing that reminds me of Helene causes a chain reaction of water accumulating in my eyes of which I cannot hold back.

> *I am weary with my groaning; all the night make*
> *I my bed to swim; I water my couch with my tears.*
> *Psalms 6:6*

Some men, not all, will not let anyone see them cry, but obviously I'm not one of them. And guess what? Neither was Jesus. Remember when Lazarus died and Jesus now found himself at his grave site ?

> *Jesus wept..... John 11:35*

We know and understand that God gave our eyes a lubricating mechanism that functions solely to keep them moist. However, let me venture to say that tears also have a spiritual "purpose."

Tears can serve as a cleansing agent for the soul.

In terms of grieving, when we allow ourselves to cry, we begin the process of healing. When we don't cry, we hold in emotions and issues that like cancer can spread and cause damage in every area of our lives. God's design in dealing with our emotions will always bring about a result that will benefit us, not destroy us. In allowing ourselves to cry, we provide access to possibly some deeply hidden issues we have been ignoring, such as guilt, anger, and bitterness, just to name a few.

None of these are healthy when kept inside of us. They must be dealt with. Because our heart is the seat of our emotions, it is imperative that we constantly guard it from those external things that will harm us.

Keep thy heart with all diligence;
for out of it are the issues of life.... Proverbs 4:23

To keep means to protect and maintain. We normally don't do a good job in preventing certain things from getting into our hearts. When we neglect properly addressing issues within our heart, they can build up and take root, causing even deeper problems. For example, simple anger can progressively turn into bitterness, wrath and then malice. Tears work in this regard by at least bringing to the forefront that something is wrong and if honestly addressed, can begin a process of cleansing and healing.

Tears can be an expression of thanksgiving and worship. Not all the tears I've shed have been in sorrow. Many times I've given praise and thanksgiving to God for what He has done. When we look in Luke 7:44, we see a woman who, no doubt, Jesus had blessed.   She shows her gratitude by washing His feet with her "tears."   It is common place to see a saint cry while in the midst of worshiping God. This is evidence of the depth of gratitude one has for what God has done or is doing in their lives. Someone even now can say "If you only knew what He's done for me, you would understand the reason for my tears."

<u>Tears can possibly change the outcome of a situation</u>. As you all may know, Helene and I became proud grandparents of twins on July 7th of 2009. Until now, I never knew that there existed a larger place in a parent's heart for their grandchildren than for their own children. I know it's coming, and those of you who are grandparents might as well say "Amen" to this fact. One of my babies is going to ask grandpa for something accompanied by a tear and will get it, even after I may have said "No" the first time. God is just like that too. You remember when King Hezekiah was about to die, he was told by the prophet to get his house in order. He prayed to God, cried, and God granted him a fifteen year extension on his life. (II Kings 20:5) The king got a reprieve (change of heart from God), and I admit that my babies will be spoiled by me — all possibly because of a "tear." Please don't misunderstand me, crying will not guarantee anything, but sometimes it can make a difference.

<u>Tears can convey a contrite, repentant and humbled spirit</u>. In cases where sin has been acknowledged and there exists a sincere attitude seeking to

be forgiven, tears can begin the process of restoration. Who among us (that understands God's grace and mercy), when approached by someone who has wronged you, would not be willing to forgive them when you have sensed sincerity, especially accompanied with tears? Do I need to remind you of what you asked God to forgive you for the other day?

Be ye kind one to another, tenderhearted,
forgiving one another,
even as God for Christ's sake has forgiven you.
Ephesians 4:32

Brokenness will make you cry. Often God has to take us to this level in order that we be reminded that we are nothing without Him.

Tears can be seeds to a harvest of blessings. God's capacity for restoring life is far beyond our capacity. Forests burn down and are able to grow back. Broken bones heal. Even grief is temporary. Our tears are seeds that will grow into a harvest of joy because God is able to bring joy out of tragedy. I know without a shadow of a doubt that God will bring me through this time. Weeping may endure for a night, but joy cometh in the morning.

They that sow in tears shall reap in joy.... Psalms 126:5

Every tear is important to God. Be aware that no matter how many tears are shed, God knows, sees and counts each one. *Put thou my tears into thy bottle; are they not in thy book? (Psalms 56:8)*

Matthew 10:30 says *"But the very hairs on your*

head are all numbered." To know that He is concerned about me, not just with what I am going through right now, but with every area in my life, is encouraging and comforting.

If you need someone to talk to, or someone to lean on, call on Jesus. However, if you just need a handkerchief, give me a call. I do have an extra one you can have.

10

Get Ready for Your Destiny

Earlier on this journey I shared with Mother Rylander about a day in which I felt so bad I didn't even come out of the house. She told me that moments still exist for her even after 15 years of her husband going home to glory.

As I now look at where God has brought me from in this short time, I'm reminded of a true story a brother told me about himself and his father. Having been disobedient to his father, the boy injured himself seriously. His father reminded him of that time, had him look at the scar that remained on his thumb, and showed that because of the healing power of God, there was no more pain. There will be "moments" that I will continue to experience just thinking about Helene. The wound that was so deep in my heart is healing from within, and a scar is beginning to appear that will forever remind me of what a remarkable, precious jewel I had in my love, my life, my Clair. However, thanks be to God... the pain is now gone.

I had believed that now the purpose of writing the book was complete. Little did I know that God was not through with me. I was awakened early one morning around 2:30 a.m., and God said to me, "Jerome, get up, I'm not done with you. There are still some things I need to show you. You need to know that I have great plans for your life. You are

about to do some things you never imagined. You
will meet some people who will bless you, and
you will touch lives far beyond your comprehen-
sion. I created you to enjoy a life of success and
greatness.   Helene, now being with me, even
though you were not ready and found it difficult to
accept, was what I needed to do in order for you to
move toward your higher calling. Your best days
are ahead of you."

As I look at great Bible characters, God used a crisis to usher them into a powerful process that
caused them to break into a successful and fruitful
life. The prophet Isaiah said in Isaiah 6:1

> *"In the year that king Uzziah died I saw*
> *also the Lord sitting upon a throne*
> *high and lifted up, and his*
> *train filled the temple"*

Every one of us has a choice when our crisis
comes: to embrace our destiny or to remain where
we are. A crisis should be a wake up call. Do not
cut the alarm off and go back to sleep. Arise and
answer the call to face the challenge and move into
your destiny. God has ordered my steps through
this moment to break every limitation that has kept
me from greatness.

My love for God and His unconditional love for
me will break fear from my life.

> *For God hath not given us the spirit of fear,*
> *but of power, and of love,*
> *and of a sound mind.*
> *II Timothy 1:7*

We must understand by personal revelation that

for us who love God and who are the called according to His "purpose," everything will turn for our good (Romans 8:28). Can we trust God during the processes of life and prepare for greater days ahead? I will not be the victim, for I am a victor. I will no longer be sad because my wife is gone. For what God did, I give Him thanks.

In everything give thanks; for this is the will
of God in Christ Jesus concerning you.
II Thessalonians 5:18

I am thankful to God for creating a uniquely beautiful woman 50 years ago who accepted her calling, understood and fulfilled her purpose, was faithful to her duties as a wife, mother, daughter, sister, friend, and most of all a sister in Christ. She glorified God by using what was given to her. For that, He was faithful to her and rewarded her faith in Him. Her destiny was fulfilled.

Therefore, victimization will not play as a tool of the enemy to keep me from my destiny of greatness in God's Kingdom. The enemy will not sabotage my mind and emotions.

My pain of yesterday will not steal my vision and destiny. I have now learned amazingly through this journey that in every painful place or crisis, God positions us to receive a golden connection. The power of God is moving to assist me in becoming everything God called me to be, even when I was in my mother's womb. My true destiny is about to be uncovered.

It was not by chance but destiny, that a Jewish

baby by the name of Moses was placed in the Nile River, raised in the house of Pharaoh as an Egyptian, and would become the deliverer of His people Israel.

It was not by chance but destiny, that a young man was born blind not because of sins that he or his parents might have done, but because Jesus would be coming by on that day in order that the power of God would be witnessed by all who were present.

It was not by chance but destiny, that a young boy would die, but on his way to the graveyard, be stopped by Jesus, raised from the dead, and given back to his mother, who was a widow.

It was not by chance but destiny, that a woman who had for 18 years suffered with an infirmity that caused her to walk bow down, but after meeting the man from Galilee, was able to walk upright.

It was not by chance but destiny, that a fish would be the first UPS carrier that would deliver the money needed in order that the disciples could pay their taxes.

It was not by chance but destiny, that the servant of a centurion soldier would suddenly, after feeling sick and near death, miraculously feel healing and strength — no doctor in sight but simply because of a word of healing spoken from the Balm of Gilead.

It was not by chance but destiny, that a certain man

would be asked for the use of his donkey that had never been ridden before but that Jesus would be the first, as He would ride it into the streets of Jerusalem.

It was not by chance but destiny, that on one particular day, that seemed like any other day for 38 long years, a lame man who had been coming to a pool in hopes of being thrown in first and physically healed, would be made whole because he met Jesus.

It was destiny that a crippled man was visited by 4 friends who knew that if they could get him in to see Jesus, he would be able to walk again.

It was destiny that the virtue of Jesus would temporarily leave Him simply because of the faith of a woman's outstretched hands touching the hem of His garment in a crowd.

It was destiny that a young Jewish lad, who participated in the stoning of one of the first deacons of the church, would later become the greatest of the apostles, even though he considered himself to be the least of them all.

It was destiny that Jesus waited a few days after hearing that His friend Lazarus had died that He would allow Lazarus's death to be the subject of the lesson that He is the resurrection and the life.

*"I am the resurrection, and the life: he that believeth in me,
though he were dead, yet shall he live:
And whosoever liveth and believeth
in me shall never die".
John 11: 25—26*

It has become a part of my destiny…...

That on August 5, 2009 at 8:53 a.m., after 28 wonderful years with the greatest wife a man could ever have, God decided to call her home, leaving me to continue my journey and fulfill my purpose for Him. I don't know what the future holds, but I do know who holds the future.

> *Not as though I have already attained, either were already perfect: but I follow after, if that I may apprehend that for which I am apprehended of Christ Jesus.*
>
> *Brethren, I count not myself to have apprehended; but this one thing I do, forgetting those things which are behind, and reaching forth unto those things which are before I press toward the mark for the prize of the high calling of God in Christ Jesus.*
> *Philippians 3: 12-14*

I will not ever forget my wife, Helene. I now look forward with great anticipation to what God has for me. Whatever it may be, to Him be all the glory, honor and praise.

Epilogue

What God Did For Me

God reaffirmed that He knows what's best for us. - God's ways are not our ways, and his thoughts are not our thoughts. He is in control of our lives and will always allow circumstances to happen for the good to those who love him. Helene, who loved God, lived for God, and whose hope was in God, is now with God. No longer will she have to experience the pain and challenges that this mortal existence brings, for now corruption has put on incorruption and mortal has put on immortality... death is now swallowed up in victory. My tears must be tears of joy, knowing that her life and hope was not in vain, but that she has been rewarded eternal life because she believed in Jesus Christ as the Son of God.

Well done, thou good and faithful servant: thou hast been faithful over a few things, I will make thee ruler over many things: enter thou into the joy of the Lord.
Matthew 25: 21

What will God say to you?

God showed me that He will use anyone and anything to accomplish His purpose. I am astonished at the multiplicity and variety of people and things God used in revealing His purpose and desire for me on this journey. I experienced God from the hug of a little child that hurt because she saw me in pain, a letter or phone call from a person I had never met, practical truths communicated through a television program, and the power of praise, just to name few. You can see God in anything if you would simply get in tune to His Spirit. *"God is a rewarder of them that dili-gently seek Him." (Hebrews 11:6)* Seek to find God in all that life may bring. Remember that He is sovereign and is in control of everything. He knows what He is doing, and if we simply trust Him, we'll see when He's through that we are bet-ter because of it.

> **Trust in the Lord with all thine heart,**
> **lean not to thy own understanding.**
> **In all thy ways acknowledge him**
> **and he shall direct thy path.**
> **Proverbs 3:5-8**

God showed me just how much He loves me and cares. - Sometimes people will never know just how much of an impact they have made on others' lives. With Helene's death, I have been tremendously blessed to be able to say that I believe her life and hopefully mine would have made a difference in someone else's life. If we leave you with nothing else, get to know Jesus as your Savior. Pour your life into the life of someone else. Each one of us has a beginning and an end. It is a blessing if one lives a long life, but that is not what is so important. Between the years you are born and die is a dash. The question I would propose to you is.... What will your dash say about you? Will it say that you loved as God loved? That you cared about others? It's not the quantity of what you have obtained in life that matters but the quality of which you lived. If I can help somebody, then I know that my life would not have been in vain. Will you be missed when you leave here? Believe me, you will be leaving here.

But God commendeth his love toward us,
in that, while we were yet sinners,
Christ died for us.
Romans 8:5

God showed me that some will have to go through hell in order for some to get to heaven. I must give credit and gratitude to my friend Pastor Gabriel Lewis for helping me see the reality of this truth. There are some experiences in life, for me the loss of Helene, that will take you to the lowest places humanly possible. For me, it was a pit. Joseph found himself in a pit. He had to go there in order to fulfill the plan of God and be used in saving his brethren and fulfilling the promise to Abraham, Isaac, and Jacob. Jesus went into the pit of hell after his death. He had to go there in order to rob death, its sting, and the grave, its victory, and rise from the grave providing us with eternal salvation. I had to experience such extreme loss (my pit) in order to better understand God's greater purpose for me and to be prepared to share with others what God can do for them when darkness enters their life.

God showed me the importance of enjoying life and those who are in my life to the fullest. I was blessed with a gift from heaven. Never take for granted the people in your life. Make the most of the time you have. Say to, as well as show those whom you love that they are precious, not only to God but also to you. You can take nothing with you. Give what you have to others. Since death can come suddenly with no warning, cherish every moment you have with the one you love.

Yesterday was a cancelled check,
Tomorrow is a promissory note,
Today is ready cash.....
spend it wisely

God showed me His displeasure in my personal level of devotion to Him. This, by far, was the most difficult and painful lesson on this journey. One morning, as I was meditating, I began to realize that the closeness I now have with God quite possibly may not have happened if Helene were still alive. I was convicted of having a complacent relationship with Him. In the midst of tears, I had to humbly seek His forgiveness. We can think in our minds that we're all right with God. It is so easy to fall into the trap of "losing your first love", causing you to have a lukewarm relationship with Him.

I was so caught up in doing "ministry" in the name of God that I had neglected spending time in relationship with Him. My mind now is constantly seeking His thoughts. My desire is, more than ever before, focused on walking in His ways. Do not ever let service for God replace personal devotion with God. I do not believe Helene's passing was a punishment to me; however, it did serve as a wake-up call to me and hopefully a warning to others not to take God for granted.

*How can two walk together
except they agree.
Amos 3:3*

I had a close relationship with Helene because we spent a lot of quality time "together." How much quality time are you spending with God? Don't let God have to do something drastic to get your attention.

God showed me that He had to "break" me, in order to "make" me. That clay in the hands of the potter has no idea what it is to become, only the potter knows. God knows the beginning and the end of our lives. Because I am still here, it is obvious that God is not through with me and that I am still under construction, being molded and made into what He wants me to be. My life up to this point had already been seen in the mind of God. What God has done has forced me to face some hard realities and fears about me. These things would not have been known had God not brought me to this place of brokenness.

It is in this place of brokenness that I have come to see God as never before. It is in this place of brokenness that I have gained a greater dependency on Him. It is in this place of brokenness that I now have a greater understanding and appreciation of the grace and mercies of God.

Through this humbling experience, I see more clearly some of the things God wants me to do. I've been challenged to believe that I can do greater things for Him. And what I do from this point on, may it all be to His glory and to His honor.

It is my prayer that your walk with me along this journey has helped you in some way. The intent of sharing with you this very personal time in my life was, as stated from the beginning, simply an act of obedience to God. I have never experienced such levels of heartache, grief, and devastation; therefore, I did not know what to expect. I needed help in coping with my pain, in making sense of my world which was suddenly falling apart. In this darkness I needed to see some light.

God said "Be honest with yourself about what you are feeling and write it down. As you saw me in every aspect of this journey, know that my purpose for it was to reassure you that I love you, wanted to heal you, and prepare you for greater things I have in store for you." In the process of being obedient, I discovered God as never before.

> *"God will take you where you need to go*
> *in order for you to become what*
> *He wants you to be."*

Pastor Jerome G. Farris

Breinigsville, PA USA
15 December 2009
229269BV00001B/1/P